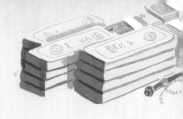

For Mia, Ayalah and Naomi

Written by Raphael Honigstein

Illustrated by Caroline Attia

The Big Book of Treasures

THE MOST AMAZING DISCOVERIES EVER MADE AND STILL TO BE MADE

LITTLE
GESTALTEN

The Whydah Gally
4

King John's Treasure
40

GREENLAND

NORTH AMERICA

The SS Gairsoppa
28

The Nuestra Señora de Atocha
88

La Noche Triste
"The Night of Sorrows"
8

The Lascaux Cave
44

SOUTH AMERICA

El Dorado
16

The Concepción
20

The Jules Rimet Trophy
24

The Treasure of th

The Archaeopteryx
52

The Amber Room
48

The Tomb of Genghis Khan
68

Brothers

36

The Fabergé Eggs

The Priam's Treasure
64

76

The Bactrian Gold

80

The Terracotta Army

60

The Menorah

92

The Rosetta Stone

AUSTRALIA

12

72

The Ark of the Covenant

84

gen

The Tomb of Tutankhamun

The Padmanabhaswamy Temple

ASIA

EUROPE

ICA

ARTICA

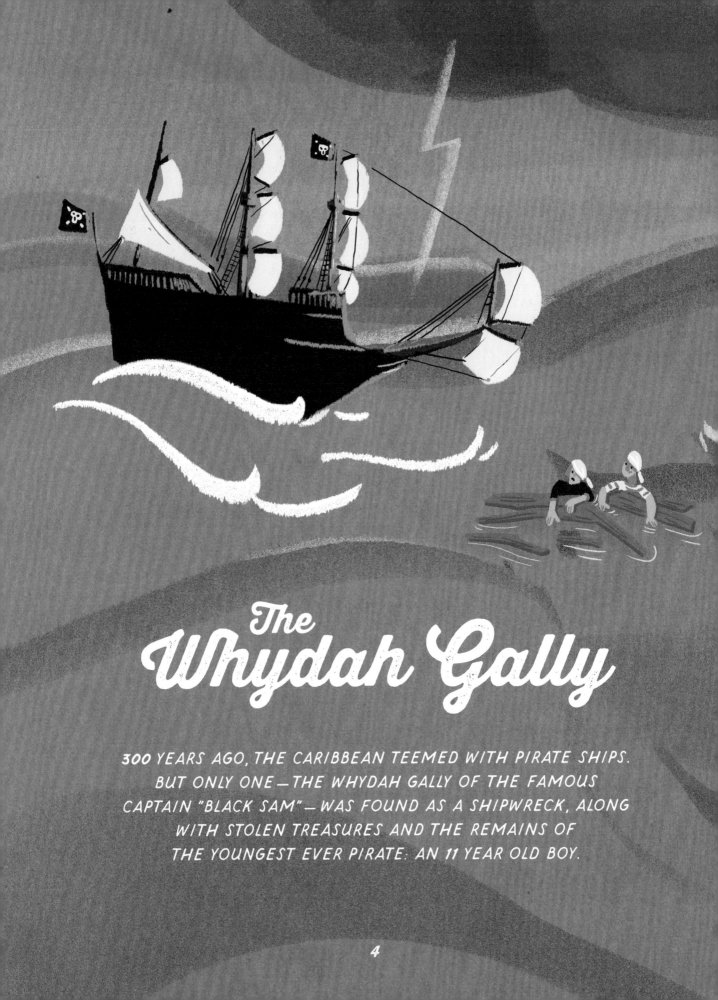

The Whydah Gally

300 YEARS AGO, THE CARIBBEAN TEEMED WITH PIRATE SHIPS.
BUT ONLY ONE — THE WHYDAH GALLY OF THE FAMOUS
CAPTAIN "BLACK SAM" — WAS FOUND AS A SHIPWRECK, ALONG
WITH STOLEN TREASURES AND THE REMAINS OF
THE YOUNGEST EVER PIRATE: AN 11 YEAR OLD BOY.

Eleven-year-old John King and his mother were passengers on a boat called Bonetta, traveling from Antigua to Jamaica on November 9, 1716, when a frightened cry went out: "Pirates!" Within no time, the famous Samuel "Black Sam" Bellamy and his crew of scoundrels captured the ship. After 15 days of looting, Black Sam, who owed his nickname to his long black hair, was ready to move on, but a little voice shouted at him to wait. "I want to join you!" demanded John. Black Sam laughed at the boy's wish. But John would not take no for an answer. He threatened to hurt his own mother if he was not allowed to go. The pirates were impressed by such terrible behavior and agreed to take John on as a crew member.

Bellamy, who had served in Britain's Royal Navy before turning into an outlaw on the seas, was incredibly good at pirating. He seized 53 boats in only one year, becoming incredibly rich in the process. "The Prince of Pirates," they called him, for he was a rather polite pirate, tidily dressed in velvet coats and well mannered. In February 1717, Black Sam pulled off his biggest coup, capturing the Whydah Gally near the Bahamas. The 112-foot-long (34-meter-long) British ship had sailed from Benin in West

THE PIRATE SHIP SAILED FROM THE CARIBBEAN TO MAINE, WHERE IT SANK NEAR CAPE COD.

Africa, with 500 slaves and precious goods onboard, to the Caribbean, where she had traded her cargo for precious metal and other supplies, such as rum, that were in high demand in England.

Black Sam made the Whydah Gally the flagship of his fleet—he commanded three ships in total—and sailed her up the American coast towards Maine, looting and capturing more vessels as he went along.

Some say Bellamy was on his way to marry the beautiful Maria Hallett, who lived in the coastal town of Eastham, Massachusetts. Her parents, the story goes, had forbidden the marriage a few years earlier, telling

Bellamy that he was not rich enough. Now he was very wealthy. But, sadly, he never got to see his lover again. The Whydah Gally became lost in thick fog off Cape Cod, was hit by a violent storm, and sank. Only two members of the 144-strong crew survived. They were tried for piracy and robbery for their troubles.

Captain Cyprian Southack, a local salvager and cartographer, made a map of the Whydah's location but little of value was recovered.

More than 200 years later, the American treasure hunter and underwater archeologist Barry Clifford used Southack's map to discover the Whydah wreck under 14 feet (4.3 meters) of water and 5 feet (1.5 meters) of sand. When the ship's engraved bell was found a year later, the Whydah became the first ever pirate shipwreck to have its identity confirmed beyond doubt. In 2016, Clifford claimed to have found most of the treasure, tons of gold and silver. He also uncovered thousands of other items of interest, including fancy belts and buttons from the pirates' extravagant clothes. Among the Whydah's artifacts, exhibited at the Whydah Pirate Museum in Provincetown today, is also a small black-leather shoe, together with a silk stocking and a leg bone, later determined to be that of a child approximately 11 years old. The old pirate tale of John King, the boy buccaneer, was proven true. ✗

Cuba

Hispaniola

JOHN KING, 11, WAS ONE OF THE YOUNGEST PIRATES EVER.

AMERICAN TREASURE HUNTER BARRY CLIFFORD FOUND THE WHYDAH IN 1984.

La Noche Triste
„The Night of Sorrows"

HUNDREDS OF SOLDIERS AND MEXICAN NATIVES DIED
WHEN SPANISH CONQUISTADOR HERNÁN CORTÉS
TRIED TO ESCAPE FROM THE AZTEC CAPITAL WITH MANY
BAGS OF STOLEN GOLD IN JULY 1520.
MOST OF THE TREASURE WAS LOST IN A LAKE.

Not long after Christopher Columbus discovered America, soldiers and explorers from Spain and Portugal came to the New World and took control of its territories by force. They were called the conquistadors. One of them, the Spaniard Hernán Cortés, led an expedition to an area populated by the Aztec tribe in modern Mexico, in 1519.

Cortés and his army of invaders and fighters from the Tlaxcaltecas tribe, who supported the Spanish, took up residence in the Aztec capital of Tenochtitlan, a city built on an island in Lake Texcoco. Aztec king Moctezuma II welcomed them with gifts of gold, which made the Spanish even greedier. Fearing an attack from the natives, Cortés took Moctezuma hostage. The Aztec ruler told his people that the gods had ordered him to live with the Spaniards at their compound, but they did not believe him and became more and more angry.

KING MOCTEZUMA OF THE AZTECS
AT FIRST WELCOMED THE
SPANISH SOLDIERS WITH LAVISH GIFTS.

CORTÉS AND HIS MEN TOOK MOCTEZUMA HOSTAGE AND HOPED TO ESCAPE WITH THE GOLD.

CORTES

HERNÁN CORTÉS, BORN IN 1485, CONQUERED MOST OF MEXICO FOR THE SPANISH CROWN.

That was not Cortés's only problem, though. The powerful governor of Cuba had sent out an army to arrest him, after Cortés had ignored his instructions. The conquistador marched his men to the coast and defeated the governor's soldiers in a bloody battle. In the meantime, Cortés's lieutenant Pedro de Alvarado—the second man in command—was becoming afraid that the natives were about to attack. While the Aztec noblemen and priests celebrated a festival in the Great Temple, Alvarado had them brutally killed. In revenge, the locals rebelled against Moctezuma's orders and encircled the compound. Nobody was allowed to leave.

Then, Moctezuma was killed. We do not exactly know how or why. The Spaniards later said the Aztecs threw rocks and poison darts at him as he addressed the crowds, but the locals told a different story: according to them, the Aztec ruler was killed by the conquistadors. Inside the compound, the supplies of food had run so low that Cortés had to come up with a plan. He told his men to break out of the city under the cover of darkness on July 1, 1520, with as much of the Aztec treasure as they could carry. The Spaniards forgot that gold is not just shiny and valuable but also very heavy, however. The weight of the loot was too much for many soldiers as they crossed over a shaky portable bridge. They perished or drowned when the Aztecs attacked them on hundreds of canoes. In total, a few hundred Spaniards and thousands of natives died in the horrific fight, and most of the gold sank to the bottom of the lake.

A wounded Cortés, who had fought his way out of the city and reached dry land, looked back at the slaughter with tears in his eyes. The awful debacle became known as the Night of Sorrows—"La Noche Triste", in Spanish—due to the lost lives and treasure. And that was not the end of the cruelty. Cortés later returned to destroy the Aztec Empire altogether. But the gold was never found. The lake was later drained and most of the basin is now taken up by Mexico City, one of the biggest cities in the world, with a population of nine million people. ✗

WHEN THE SPANISH TRIED TO FLEE WITH THE TREASURE, A TERRIBLE BATTLE ENSUED.

The Tomb of Tutankhamun

IN 1922, BRITISH ARCHEOLOGIST HOWARD CARTER UNEARTHED ONE OF THE MOST IMPORTANT HISTORICAL ARTIFACTS EVER FOUND: THE LARGELY INTACT TOMB OF TUTANKHAMUN, TOGETHER WITH HUNDREDS OF OBJECTS FROM ANCIENT EGYPT. BUT DID THE PHARAOHS CAST A DEADLY SPELL IN REVENGE?

London-born Howard Carter was only 17 years old when he started excavating the tombs of pharaohs in 1891. Thanks to financial backing from Lord Carnarvon, an English aristocrat fascinated by Ancient Egypt, Carter was allowed to explore the Valley of the Kings, an area near the Nile River where many of Egypt's rulers were buried. In Roman times and even before, masses of tourists from near and far had traveled to the valley to marvel at the tombs inside the rocks. Some of them had scribbled their names into the stone to mark their visit.

For a long time, however, Carter found nothing of interest. The known tombs had all been plundered by grave robbers many thousands of years ago. Just as he was about to give up, he noticed a flight of stones underneath old workers' huts in November 1922. They led to a door marked with hieroglyphics bearing the name of pharaoh Tutankhamun.

Carter sent a telegraph—an early version of an email, transmitted via telephone lines—to Lord Carnarvon in London, waited for him to arrive, and then made a small hole in the door with a chisel that his grandmother had given him for his 17th birthday. "Can you see anything?" Carnarvon asked. Carter replied with the famous words: "Yes, wonderful things!"

Robbers had removed some things shortly after Tutankhamun's burial

LORD CARNARVON AND HIS DAUGHTER, LADY EVELYN HERBERT, WITNESSED THE OPENING OF THE TOMB.

13

3,500 years ago, but Carter could see statues of strange animals representing Egyptian gods and hundreds of artifacts, including four chariots the pharaoh had used (one for hunting, one for war, two for parades to show off his wealth) and a chest containing his walking stick, weapons, a copper trumpet—the oldest brass instrument ever found—and even his royal underpants.

But then strange things started happening. Carter's pet canary was eaten by a cobra. The local workers were afraid that it was a sign of bad fortune. In April 1923, Carnarvon died after a mosquito bite had become infected. Other people who had entered the tomb passed away under mysterious circumstances, too. Newspapers speculated that they had all fallen victim to a curse of the pharaohs as revenge for disturbing their peace. But Carter dismissed these stories as silly superstition. He continued to explore and eventually found the body of Tutankhamun, preserved as a mummy with bandages, inside three coffins, and a beautiful mask made from solid gold and precious stones.

Tutankhamun, as it turned out, was only nine years old when he became king of Egypt in 1332 BC, and died aged 19, probably from malaria, a disease transmitted by mosquitos. He had injured his left foot and was not able to walk without a cane. King Tut could have done with some braces, too, because he had a very bad overbite. But they did not have orthodontists in those days.

A further 7,000 objects, including wine jars, ointments, and a statute of Anubis, the god of the afterlife, were found in adjacent rooms up until 1932. No one else has ever discovered such a complete Egyptian tomb or historical treasures of such significance. Two possible undiscovered chambers might harbor more wonderful things, but they are yet to be opened by the Egyptian authorities. ✗

FOUR OF THE PHARAOH'S CHARIOTS WERE FOUND, AND EVEN HIS UNDERPANTS.

KING TUT'S RESTING PLACE WAS FOUND BENEATH WORKERS' HUTS.

SIR WALTER RALEIGH WAS ONE OF
MANY EUROPEAN ADVENTURERS WHO TRIED —
AND FAILED — TO FIND THE GOLDEN CITY.

El Dorado

EUROPEAN ADVENTURERS SPENT *200* YEARS SEARCHING FOR A LOST CITY MADE OF GOLD IN SOUTH AMERICA BUT FOUND THAT NOT ALL THAT GLITTERS IS ACTUALLY REAL ...

The legend of El Dorado, Spanish for "the Golden," started with different tales that became part of the same myth over the course of time. When the conquistadors—European explorers and soldiers attracted to the riches of the New World—first met natives wearing jewelry made from gold and silver in the early sixteenth century, they naturally wondered where all that precious metal came from. Rumors of a "golden king," a tribal chief covered in gold from head to toe, and of a secret golden city overflowing with riches started a huge treasure hunt. Adventurers from Germany, Spain, and England scoured the northeast of the continent, in an area between today's Brazil, Venezuela, and Guyana, on the lookout for a place called Manoa, next to Lake Parima. That was the source of all the gold, the conquistadors believed. Nobody knew exactly where Manoa

THE MUISCA TRIBE'S HABIT OF THROWING GOLDEN ARTIFACTS INTO A LAKE BECAME PART OF THE EL DORADO LEGEND.

and Lake Parima were, but that did not stop people including them both on official maps as if their existence was beyond doubt. These were copied many times and brought back to Europe, where even more soldiers of fortune became excited about the promise of a golden city.

The Spaniards Gonzalo Pizarro and Francisco de Orellana thought they would strike it rich in what is Ecuador today. No sign of El Dorado there—but they discovered the mighty Amazon River and named it after a tribe of female warriors who had attacked the expedition. These feisty women, who fought with bows and arrows, reminded Orellana of the Amazons, female warriors described in books from ancient Greece.

Sir Walter Raleigh, an English nobleman, twice sailed to South America to find El Dorado. The embellished stories of his journeys did much to spread the idea of a golden city, but his luck ran out. After his return to England, King James I had him beheaded at London's Palace of Westminster in 1618 for breaking the peace treaty with Spain. Raleigh's

THE EUROPEANS' GREED LED TO MUCH BLOODSHED.

18

men had looted a Spanish camp on the Orinoco river (in Guyana) for supplies.

Others, meanwhile, were looking for the Muisca tribe in Colombia. The chief of the Muisca, some earlier explorers had reported, conducted a religious ceremony covered in gold dust and threw pieces of gold into Lake Guatavita. Spanish soldiers captured lots of gold from the Muisca and were told about the ritual at the lake, but expeditions to the surrounding areas turned up nothing. Lake Guatavita was later drained but pro-

vided no significant finds, either. After silver mines (in Peru) and gold mines (in Brazil) were discovered, the pursuit of El Dorado lost much of its appeal. In the 1970s, Brazilian scientists found some evidence that a lake once existed in the area where the conquistadors had looked for Lake Parima, but it is now widely accepted that there never was a city made of gold. When somebody speaks of "El Dorado" today, they often use it as a phrase to describe a fruitless search for riches by men or women who are blinded by greed. ✗

LAKE GUAVITA WAS SAID TO CONTAIN MOUNTAINS OF GOLD BUT LITTLE OF IT WAS FOUND.

Cuba

The Concepción

WILLIAM PHIPS WAS A LITTLE BOY WITH A BIG DREAM:
HE WANTED TO FIND SHIPWRECK GOLD. AND WITH
THE HELP OF THE KING OF ENGLAND AND A SURVIVOR FROM
A SUNKEN SPANISH GALLEON, HIS WISH CAME TRUE.

In September 1641, a fleet of 30 Spanish ships laden with silver and gold coins set sail from Havana, Cuba, headed for Spain. A few days into the treacherous journey, a terrible hurricane struck. The flagship, a galleon called Nuestra Señora de la Pura y Limpia Concepción, suffered the worst damage. She lost her mast and was unable to navigate.

The Concepción ran aground on a reef north of Hispaniola (the Dominican Republic and Haiti today), and was then hit by a second storm to make matters worse. The admiral and some officers escaped in the only longboat, but the vast majority of the 300-strong crew was left behind. Some made rafts from the wreckage and survived. Many did not.

Hispaniola

WILLIAM PHIPS WAS
A POOR SHEPHERD
BEFORE HE FOUND
THE CONCEPCIÓN'S TREASURE.

A DIVING BELL WAS USED
TO LOOK FOR THE WRECK NEAR
THE TURKS AND CAICOS ISLANDS.

There were lots of sharks in the seas. Attempts to salvage the ship's cargo, more than 100 tons of precious metal, were made by Spain and various adventurers. But they all looked in the wrong place. None of the survivors were able to describe the ship's exact location.

A few years later, a poor, fatherless boy from New England (Maine, USA, today) imagined that he could one day find shipwreck treasure while he tended the family's sheep. His name was William Phips. Phips grew up to be a carpenter and later found work in a Boston shipyard. In 1675, he set up his own shipyard, and five years later, he was rich enough to embark on a treasure hunt in the Bahamas with the support of King James II of England. Phips discovered a few shipwrecks that yielded a few gold coins. But his most amazing find was an actual survivor of the sunken Concepción in a port tavern. The sailor claimed he knew where the galleon had sunk and drew a map for Phips. In London, Phips and the Duke of Albemarle, who loved a bit of fun, raised money for another expedition to the Caribbean. They set up a company with the permission of James II, who demanded 10 percent of any finds for the crown. Phips sailed towards Hispaniola with two ships, the James and Mary and the Henry

IN 1978, AMERICAN TREASURE HUNTER BURT WEBBER, FOUND ANOTHER PART OF THE SHIP – AND EVEN MORE GOLD.

of London, in September 1686. The treasure map pointed to a reef called Ambrosia Banks, in an area between today's Dominican Republic and the Turks and Caicos Islands. Phips arrived there in December 1686, and one month later, one of the divers from the Henry found a ship's cannon buried on the ocean bed. It was the Nuestra Señora! Using a contraption called a diving bell, a metal chamber that allowed divers to breathe in deep waters, Phips's men spent three months raising more than 34 tons of coins, precious metal pieces, and silver bars, worth a tidy 63 million dollars (50 million pounds) in today's money. The dream had come true. Phips returned to London as a hero, and was made a knight by King James II. His success

inspired many other British treasure hunters to try their luck, all backed by rich investors. Most of them came back empty handed, however. So much money was lost that the London stock market, where parts of treasure-hunting companies were bought and sold, crashed in 1694. The story of the Concepción was not over yet, though.

300 years after Phips's discovery, the American treasure hunter Burt Webber managed to find a different part of the wreck with the help of a magnetometer and the logbook from the Henry, which he had unearthed in an old library in Maidstone, England. Webber salvaged another 60,000 coins, bullion pieces, and gold chains, worth 80 million dollars (62 million pounds) in today's money. ✗

The Jules Rimet Trophy

IN 1966, FOOTBALL'S BIGGEST PRIZE, THE WORLD CUP TROPHY, WAS STOLEN IN LONDON. THE POLICE CAUGHT THE THIEF BUT DID NOT RECOVER THE CUP—UNTIL A FOUR-LEGGED FRIEND CAME TO THE RESCUE.

Three months before the start of the 1966 World Cup in England, the Jules Rimet Trophy (named after a former president of FIFA, football's governing body) was on show in a public exhibition at Westminster Central Hall in London. Five uniformed officers kept careful watch on the cup, which was made from silver and covered with a thin layer of gold. But on Sundays, the guard closest to the glass cabinet that housed the trophy had his day off. While the other four were on a break, maybe drinking tea or using the bathroom, somebody broke through the back door, opened the display case, and disappeared with the golden booty. What a kerfuffle! How could there be a Football World Cup without the World Cup for the winners? Detective Inspector Bill Little from Scotland Yard started investigating. Nobody had seen the theft, but two

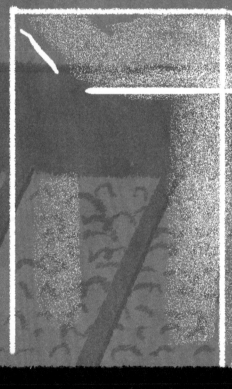

A MYSTERIOUS "MR JACKSON" CONTACTED FOOTBALL ASSOCIATION CHAIRMAN JOE MEARS AND ASKED FOR A RANSOM.

SIXTEEN TEAMS FROM THREE CONTINENTS COMPETED AT THE TOURNAMENT IN ENGLAND IN JULY 1966.

Joe Mears

The Evening News

witnesses reported a suspicious man hanging around by the hall's toilets. The next day, Joe Mears, the chairman of English football team Chelsea FC and of the Football Association, received a phone call. A man calling himself "Mr. Jackson" told him that a package "with instructions" for retrieving the cup would soon arrive at Chelsea's Stamford Bridge. It contained the lining from inside the Jules Rimet Trophy and a ransom demand made from cut out newspaper letters. The cup would go to the "scrapyard" if Mears did not pay 15,000 pounds in one- and five-pound notes and not tell the police, it threatened.

Jackson called Mears again to check he had received the package and promised to send the cup by taxi on Saturday if the money was handed over the day before. If Mears agreed, he should place an ad in the "London Evening News" with the message "Willing to do business Joe." Mears did. And he also informed Detective Inspector Len Buggle, who had taken over the case from Little.
Buggle pretended to be an assistant of the FA boss and picked up Jackson in Mears's brown Ford Zodiac at the meeting point at Battersea Park. He handed over a suitcase filled with real money at the top and bottom but only paper in the middle. Jackson told him to drive around for a few minutes. But then he spotted a van following and suspected it was the police. Jackson told Buggle to stop the car and dashed out, with Buggle giving

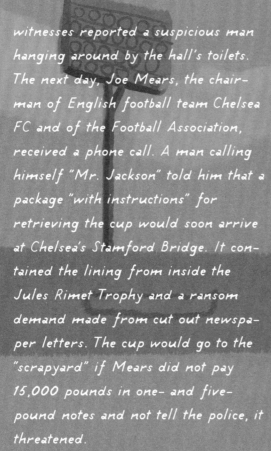

FOUR-YEAR-OLD COLLIE PICKLES (AND HIS OWNER, DAVID CORBETT) FOUND THE WORLD CUP AFTER THE FAILED BLACKMAIL ATTEMPT.

WE WAnT 15000£ FOr thE tROPHY

chase. A short pursuit ended with Jackson getting arrested in the garden of a house.

But where was the World Cup? Jackson, who turned out to be a petty thief once called Edward Bletchley that had once been convicted of handling stolen tins of corned beef, refused to give up the trophy's location. The police and the tournament organizers were getting very worried. On March 27, exactly one week after the cup had been taken, David Corbett went to make a telephone call from a kiosk outside his home in Norwood, in South London. Pickles, his four-year-old dog, accompanied him on the short walk. The collie had originally belonged to Corbett's brother John but had been passed on to David because he had the unwelcome habit of chewing furniture. Pickles stopped at a garden hedge. He started sniffing. Something was there, wrapped in newspaper. Corbett picked up the bundle, peeked inside, and could not believe his eyes: the World Cup! Pickles became a national hero after sparing the authorities' blushes. Together with his owner—who received a 5,000-pound reward—he attended the festive dinner after England's 4-2 win over Germany at the final in Wembley Stadium and a little later starred in a film called "The Spy with a Cold Nose." ✗

The SS Gairsoppa

A GERMAN SUBMARINE SANK THE BRITISH CARGO STEAMSHIP SS GAIRSOPPA WITH A TORPEDO IN 1941. TONS OF SILVER WORTH MILLIONS SEEMED LOST FOREVER AT THE BOTTOM OF THE DEEP IRISH SEA, BUT MODERN TECHNOLOGY MADE IT POSSIBLE TO RECOVER THE TREASURE.

The 410-foot-long (125-meter-long) SS Gairsoppa, named after beautiful waterfalls in southwest India, was a cargo steamship carrying vital supplies from Asia to Great Britain during the Second World War. Her last voyage began in the Indian city of Kolkata in December 1940. Loaded with a few thousand tons of valuable items—iron, tea, and many silver bars—the Gairsoppa joined up with SL-64, a convoy of British merchant ships in Freetown, Sierra Leone (West Africa), and headed for the port city of Liverpool in England. The plan was to join up with another convoy (HG-53) that was protected by two war ships of the Royal Navy. But

before the Gairsoppa reached them, a
German submarine, one of the feared
U-boats, destroyed seven ships in
February 1941. The Gairsoppa,
hampered by its heavy cargo and bad
weather, had to break off from the
other vessels in SL-64 to head for
Galway Harbor in Ireland, a country
that was neutral during the war. The
coal that powered her steam engine
had run so low that reaching
Liverpool was no longer possible.
An enemy aircraft, a German Focke-
Wulf Fw 200, spotted the Gairsoppa on
the morning of February 16 and cir-
cled around her. Later that night, the
German U-101 submarine, commanded
by Captain Ernst Mengersen, fired

four torpedoes. One hit the Gairsoppa on the starboard side (the right side, facing forward). The explosion ripped a huge hole in the cargo hold. Water flooded in, and it did not take long for the ship to sink—300 miles (500 kilometers) off the Irish coast.

Of the 85 crew members, only one, Second Officer R.H. Ayres, survived, reaching the shore after nearly two weeks on the icy open sea in a lifeboat. The others drowned or died from machine-gun fire from the U-boat. For decades, it was considered impossible to lift the Gairsoppa's precious cargo from the seabed of the

SPECIAL 50 PENCE COINS WERE MADE FROM SOME OF THE RECOVERED SILVER.

treacherous North Atlantic. The ship had gone down in waters nearly 3 miles (5 kilometers) deep. That is the combined height of 49 Big Ben clock towers—or 1,073 double-decker buses. But advances in technology, namely the invention of a low-frequency sonar system that can send sound waves into waters thousands of meters deep, and remote-controlled diving robots capable of picking up heavy metal, encouraged the British government to offer a tempting deal: anyone who could salvage the Gairsoppa's silver treasure could keep 80 percent for themselves. U.S. company Odyssey Marine Explorations, experts in finding shipwrecks, was awarded the license. They discovered the Gairsoppa's location in September 2011. Two years later, they had recovered almost all of the silver, 2,792 bars weighing 36 kilograms each, with an estimated value of 171 millions dollars (132 million pounds). In 2014, the Royal Mint issued 20,000 commemorative 50 pence coins, struck using a portion of the Gairsoppa silver, the heaviest and deepest shipwreck treasure ever found. ✗

300 MILES (600 KILOMETERS) OFF THE IRISH COAST, THE GAIRSOPPA WAS SUNK. ONLY ONE CREW MEMBER SURVIVED.

IRELAND

✗ GALWAY

✗ SS GAIRSOPPA

ERICH (LEFT) AND FRANZ SASS
WERE GANGSTERS WHO LOVED THE GOOD LIFE.

THE SASS BROTHERS WERE SMART.
THEY USED BLOW TORCHES
TO CUT THROUGH SAFE DOORS.

The Sass Brothers

ERICH AND FRANZ SASS WERE THE MOST FAMOUS BANK BURGLARS IN GERMANY JUST OVER 100 YEARS AGO, ADMIRED FOR OUTWITTING THE POLICE AND FOR GIVING STOLEN MONEY TO POOR PEOPLE. BUT WHERE IS THE BOOTY FROM THEIR MOST DARING HEIST?

Detective sergeant Max Fabich had just polished off a lovely schnitzel—some say it was actually a portion of grilled sausages, but that does not really matter—in a café in Berlin's Grunewald park when he saw a familiar face emerge from behind a bush: it was Erich Sass, the master thief! Erich was carrying a shovel and looked dirty. Very, very suspicious,

Fabich thought. He had tried to bring Erich and his brother Franz to justice for years. But these two "gentleman gangsters," as the newspapers called them, had always been too smart to get caught. Had they buried the loot of their biggest coup in the middle of Grunewald park?

The two Sass brothers grew up in Moabit, a poor area of Germany's

professional criminals, using a blow-torch to cut through the doors of safes. But their first four attempts all failed. Once, a cleaner surprised them. On another occasion, they accidentally set a crate of money on fire and had to run away.

On January 30, 1929, the cashier of the Disconto Bank could not open the heavy safe door, which had been jammed from the inside. It took three days for workers to smash through a wall to gain access to the ransacked vault. 179 empty deposit boxes littered the floor and hundreds of thousands of Reichsmark and foreign currency notes belonging to the city's wealthiest people had been stolen, along with jewelry, gold, and an antique work given to a German Navy admiral by the Sultan of Zanzibar.

The Sass brothers had broken into an adjacent basement, tunneled through two walls, and climbed into a ventilation shaft that led directly into the vault. Nobody had noticed the ploy;

capital, living together in a small apartment with two more brothers (Max and Hans) and their parents. Erich, the small and clever one, and his much taller brother Franz started stealing from warehouses when they were still in school. Later, they became

THE BROTHERS DUG TUNNELS TO GET INTO BANKS AND GAVE SOME OF THE STOLEN MONEY TO NEIGHBORS.

as luck would have it, the bank's attentive guard dog had been banished to the back of the house after neighbors had complained about his incessant barking.

Detective Fabich discovered two golden coins, tools, and leather gloves hidden in the Sass brothers' apartment. After a couple of months in prison, they were let go: not enough evidence. Franz and Erich celebrated their release at a press conference at an expensive restaurant, cheekily sipping champagne. "We've had offers from Hollywood to turn this story into a film!" their lawyer exclaimed. In the coming months, they traveled around Germany in a yellow limousine, staying in the nicest hotels, wearing the most fashionable clothes. All over Moabit, people found money stuffed in their post boxes. The Sass brothers were adored as heroes.

In the autumn of 1933, there were suddenly many break-ins at banks in Copenhagen, Denmark.

The Sass brothers had moved country. But they were caught by the Danish police and sent back to Germany after a few years in prison. In March 1940, Franz and Erich Sass were killed by the Nazis, who did not much care for popular thieves. The booty from the Disconto break-in was never found, however. To this day, amateur treasure hunters regularly gather in Grunewald park with metal detectors to search for the Sass brothers' hidden fortune. ✗

POLICE IN DENMARK CAUGHT THEM AND SENT THEM BACK TO GERMANY, WHERE THEY WERE KILLED.

DANEMARK ✗

Berlin ✗

GERMANY

The Fabergé Eggs

FROM *1885* TO *1917*, MASTER GOLDSMITH PETER CARL FABERGÉ PRODUCED *50* INCREDIBLY BEAUTIFUL EASTER EGGS CONTAINING MINIATURE SURPRISES FOR TWO RUSSIAN EMPERORS. THEY ARE WORTH MILLIONS NOW, BUT SIX OF THEM HAVE VANISHED OVER THE YEARS AND STILL AWAIT DISCOVERY.

THE EGGS CONTAINED SURPRISES, SUCH AS A TINY GOLDEN HEN.

Russian tsar Alexander III wanted to make his wife, the empress Maria Feodorovna, a very special gift to celebrate the 20th anniversary of their engagement in 1885. He commissioned jeweler Peter Carl Fabergé to make a golden Easter egg. Easter is the most important holiday of the year—more important than Christmas, even—for the Russian Orthodox Church. The first imperial Easter egg was made from a white shell with a gold "yolk" inside. The yolk opened to reveal a hen as a surprise, and the hen in turn contained a minute diamond replica of the Russian Imperial Crown from which a small ruby pendant egg was suspended.

Unlike the surprise eggs you can buy in the supermarket today, the Fabergé eggs did not come with a tasty layer of chocolate. Nevertheless, Empress Maria was so happy with her present that the royal court jeweler was instructed to fashion an egg every Easter. The tradition was continued by Alexander and Maria's son Nicholas II, who presented an egg every year to both his wife, Alexandra Feodorovna, and his mother. The intricate surprises ranged from a perfect miniature replica of a coronation carriage—the golden horse-drawn coach that took Fabergé's employees 15 months to make—to a mechanical swan, an ivory elephant, and a heart-shaped frame on

AFTER THE RUSSIAN REVOLUTION IN 1917, THE TSAR WAS DEPOSED AND THE PALACE LOOTED.

an easel with 11 miniature portraits of members of the imperial family. Most of them, as you can guess, had beards. Ordinary people were too poor to afford such lavish gifts. Anger with the emperor was growing at the end of the First World War, which had brought hardship and hunger to Russia. In February 1917, a rebellion forced Nicholas II to abdicate the throne, and a second revolution, led by Vladimir Lenin, resulted in the looting of the imperial palaces and the transfer of the Russian capital from St. Petersburg to Moscow. Some of the 50 imperial eggs were sold to European collectors to raise money for the communist state, but seven eggs disappeared altogether. Until ... a scrap-metal dealer from the American Midwest came across a newspaper article on the internet with a photo of one of the lost eggs in 2012. It looked exactly like the golden one he had bought at a flea market for just over 13,000 dollars (10,000

pounds) about 10 years earlier. The dealer had wanted to melt it down and sell on the gold and its big diamond, but he suddenly realized this could be one of the Fabergé eggs! Kieran McCarthy, an expert from London, flew out to the scrap dealer's modest home, next to a highway and donut shop, and found that the piece in question was indeed one of the missing imperial eggs.

"I have been around the most marvelous discoveries in the art world, but I don't think I've ever seen one quite like this—finding this extraordinary treasure in the middle of nowhere was like finding Tutankhamun in Tesco," McCarthy said. The gold egg, which contained a women's watch as the surprise, was brought to Britain for a sum close to 25 million dollars (20 million pounds).

So keep an eye out. Six of these jewelry masterpieces are yet be found. ✘

NORTH SEA

SPALDING

WISBECH

KING'S LYNN

KING JOHN'S VALUABLES WERE LOST BETWEEN KING'S LYNN AND SPALDING IN EAST ANGLIA.

ENGLISH NOBLEMEN FOUGHT AGAINST THE RULE OF KING JOHN IN THE 13TH CENTURY.

King John's Treasure

ENGLAND, 1216. A TIME OF CIVIL WAR. BARONS AND KNIGHTS WERE REBELLING. KING JOHN, SUFFERING FROM A LIFE-THREATENING ILLNESS, WAS FIGHTING A DESPERATE BATTLE. LOSING HIS CROWN JEWELS DID NOT HELP ...

In the legend of Robin Hood, a medieval tale popularized by American children's book author Howard Pyle in 1883, King John is the evil baddie who steals from the poor and hunts the hero Robin Hood, who steals from the rich to give to the poor.

The real King John, who lived from 1166 to 1216 was not quite as bad by all accounts. Yes, he liked women a little too much—especially those belonging to other men. He also did not have much luck in war and constantly asked his underlings for more funds to pay for soldiers. But his greatest mistake was simply a result of bad luck. More of that later, though.

King John's reign began in 1199 after the death of his older brother, Richard the Lionheart. King John was

MAGNA
CHARTA CVMSTATV

March 1714

THE MAGNA CARTA WAS SIGNED
IN 1215 TO MAKE PEACE
BETWEEN THE KING AND REBEL KNIGHTS.

immediately forced to wage war in northern France, where his nephew Arthur I also had claims on the English throne. Historians believe Arthur I was eventually murdered by John, but John's first military campaign failed. Philip II of France conquered the region of Normandy, and England lost most of its territories on the continent.

Back home, King John had more worries. The barons and noblemen he relied on for money and military support had had enough of his demands. King John signed the Magna Carta, an important peace treaty that granted the noblemen liberties, such as the protection from illegal imprisonment. But the knights were still not happy. They invited the French prince Louis to land an army in England to take over the throne. A civil war ensued.

John realized the danger he was in. On October 12, 1216, he rushed from King's Lynn in Norfolk to Spalding, Lincolnshire, to organize his troops. Suffering from dysentery, a very, very bad case of a tummy ache, John had to cross the Wash, a treacherous area that was only passable at low tide. The king made it to safety but his baggage train, laden with the crown jewels, many gold coins, and other valuable artifacts, was apparently too slow to escape the incoming water. It got submerged or sank into the quicksand. John succumbed to his illness a week later and died.

Historians are not totally convinced that John's treasure really went missing that way—some say he could have secretly sold it to raise money—but treasure hunters have never stopped looking for what would be the greatest archeological prize ever found in England. If the crown jewels did get lost there, they are buried under 20 feet (six meters) of soil, possibly under a village, because the Wash has long since been drained to become very fertile farmland.

Recently, laser technology that can show water deposits underneath the earth—such as former swamps—has provided a good clue as to how the Norfolk coastline would have looked 800 years ago. But it will probably take the development of more powerful metal detectors, able to penetrate deep into the soil, to discover King John's lost treasure. An estimated value of 87 million dollars (70 million pounds) for the lot might provide some incentive. ✗

KING JOHN'S LOST TREASURE IS SAID TO INCLUDE THE CROWN JEWELS AND MANY OTHER VALUABLE BELONGINGS

THOUSANDS OF ANIMALS WERE PAINTED ON THE WALLS BY HUMANS LIVING IN THE LATE STONE AGE.

The Lascaux Cave

IN THE WOODLANDS OF MONTIGNAC, IN THE SOUTHWEST OF FRANCE, A STONE AGE CAVE THAT WAS UNDISTURBED FOR 17,000 YEARS BOASTS THE MOST AMAZING PREHISTORIC PAINTINGS.

Stories that start with a dog running after a rabbit rarely end well. But this one does. On September 8, 1940, Robot, the terrier in question, chased a bunny through the woods outside the French village of Montignac, all the way to a hole in the ground that turned out to be an opening to a large cave. Robot's owner, the 17-year-old apprentice car mechanic Marcel Ravidat and his three friends could barely believe their eyes when they returned the next day with a torch. They had been hoping to find a treasure that was supposedly buried somewhere in the area. But instead, they cast light upon thousands of beautifully rendered, detailed prehistoric animals—bulls, stags, horses, big cats, birds, and bears—and human figures that artists from the Late Stone Age had painted on the walls approximately 17,000 years ago.

THE CAVE WAS FOUND WHEN ROBOT, A DOG, CHASED A RABBIT DOWN A HOLE IN 1940.

These early modern humans—our direct ancestors—used paints made from minerals and animal fat to depict scenes of hunting, as well as more abstract images. The exact purpose of these paintings is not known. Maybe it was done to record previous experiences, like a photo album. Maybe they were meant to have a ritual meaning, designed to bring luck. Or maybe the people who lived and visited the cave simply enjoyed looking at them, like people who go to art galleries today.

The region around Montignac had long been known to contain caves with similar paintings, but, unlike the ones in the sealed Lascaux cave, their colors had badly faded. But here, water had never penetrated the cave, and the small hole that Robot found had only appeared a few months before, after a storm had ripped out a tree and taken off a layer of earth.

Ravidat and his mates were so overwhelmed by their discovery that they took turns keeping watch and only told one of their teachers after seven days had passed. Later, members of the French Resistance, brave men and women who fought against the occupation of France by the Germans during the Second World War, used the cave to hide their weapons. It took until 1948 before the cave and its stunning paintings—the finest Stone Age artworks ever found—was opened to the public.

Up to 2,000 visitors turned up every day to marvel at the ancient animals, but their breathing, the dirt from their shoes, the humidity, and the

FOR 17,000 YEARS, NOBODY HAD SEEN THE PAINTINGS. AN EXACT REPLICA IS OPEN TO THE PUBLIC TODAY.

Dordogne

PÉRIGUEUX

LASCAUX

light that came into the cave all started to damage the artwork. Nasty crystals and mold appeared on the walls. A special ventilation system was installed but did not make things better. The authorities were forced to close the cave in 1963. Only a few scientists were allowed in, once a week or so.

The fantastic depictions can still be seen, however. An exact replica called Lascaux II was constructed not far from the original cave. It features a 3D cinema, an interactive gallery, and a workshop for those who want to create their own wall art. Robot would be very proud. ✗

The Amber Room

THE AMBER ROOM WAS THE MOST BEAUTIFUL ROOM OF BERLIN'S CITY PALACE IN THE EARLY SEVENTEENTH CENTURY. IT WAS LOST—OR DESTROYED—DURING THE SECOND WORLD WAR 200 YEARS LATER. THE SEARCH FOR IT CONTINUES TO THIS DAY.

Some trees and other plants give off a sticky, honey-like liquid that protects them against pesky insects who want to take a bite. When this liquid hardens over the course of many millions of years, it turns into amber, a gemstone that people use in jewelry and decoration. Königsberg, a city on the Baltic coast, used to be the center of amber production in Europe—very useful for the Prussian king Frederick William I, who was born there and happened to love the shiny stuff. Frederick had an entire room of amber, gold panels, and mirrors installed in his City Palace in Berlin, the Prussian capital in 1713.

Three years later, the Russian tsar Peter the Great took a liking to the room on a visit and negotiated a trade: he sent Frederick some tall soldiers for his personal guard and took home the Amber Room in exchange. The deal helped to secure an alliance between Russia and Prussia against their northern neighbors, Sweden.
The Amber Room was moved to the Catherine Palace in Pushkin, outside St. Petersburg, by Peter the Great's granddaughter Tsarina Elisabeth because the

Russian royal family enjoyed looking at it during their summer holidays there. The room was also enlarged until it covered 600 square feet (55 square meters)—roughly the size of a school classroom. Its glory was unperturbed for over 200 years.

But then darkness engulfed Europe during the Second World War. German forces invaded St. Petersburg, which had been renamed Leningrad, in 1941 and they went straight for the Amber Room. The Russians had tried to hide it behind an ordinary-looking wallpaper, but that trick did not work. The Germans took the room apart and carried it back in boxes to Königsberg for safe-keeping in the cellars of the town's castle.

Four years later, as the war was coming to an end, Britain's Royal Air Force dropped bombs on Königsberg and damaged parts of the castle. In April 1945, the Red Army of the Soviet Union (as Russia was known at the time) destroyed the castle even further. But what had happened to the Amber Room?

The victorious Red Army found almost no trace of the six tons of amber and 129 mosaic panels in the ruins of Königsberg. Rumors surfaced that the Germans had sent away the crates of amber before the Soviets' arrival, but searches in various locations failed to throw up anything, and there was also no hard evidence that the Amber Room was loaded onto a ship that sank after being torpedoed by a Soviet submarine in the Baltic Sea, as some eyewitnesses claimed. Königsberg Castle, meanwhile, was flattened completely in 1968, which made it impossible to probe any further.

In 1997, two pieces from the Amber Room, a stone mosaic and a chest of drawers, turned up in Germany and were given back to Russia by the German government. A faithful reconstruction of the room in Catherine Palace with 350 different shades of amber took 24 years to complete, finishing up in 2003. Most people believe that the original Amber Room was destroyed in the war. But some treasure hunters have not stopped looking, hopeful that the most amazing room ever built remains hidden in boxes in the cellars of some German castle or underneath the Königsberg Cathedral. ✖

BRITISH BOMBERS DESTROYED PARTS OF THE CASTLE HOUSING THE AMBER ROOM IN 1945.

GERMAN SOLDIERS STOLE THE AMBER ROOM FROM LENINGRAD IN 1941.

The Archaeopteryx
(The London Specimen)

IN THE NINETEENTH CENTURY, THE DISCOVERY OF THE PRESERVED REMAINS OF A 147-MILLION-YEAR-OLD ANIMAL CAUSED A SENSATION. IT PROVED THAT BIRDS HAD EVOLVED FROM DINOSAURS.

EVOLUTION -

THE ARCHAEOPTERYX WAS THE MISSING LINK BETWEEN DINOSAURS AND BIRDS

Häberlein

Darwin

THE COLLECTION OF FOSSILS OF KARL HÄBERLEIN SHOWED THAT CHARLES DARWIN'S THEORY OF EVOLUTION WAS RIGHT.

In Solnhofen, Bavaria, there are large deposits of limestone, a light, hard rock that has been used as a building material since Roman times. The limestone in Solnhofen is not only very pretty but also very old. It was formed 140 to 160 million years ago—when dinosaurs lived in Europe. Some of them died and were covered by mud before their bodies fell apart or were eaten by scavengers. Over the course of many years, their bones became part of the stone itself. Remains of animals or plants preserved that way are called fossils.
In 1861, a fossilized imprint of a feather was found in Solnhofen. It must have belonged to a very old bird. That same year, a strange-looking skeleton, with bird-like wings but claws and a long, bony tail like a dinosaur, was discovered in the same area. Some people were so confused by the creature that they believed it to be the remains of an angel. But scientists concluded that both fossils were of the same ancient animal and called it Archaeopteryx, Greek for "ancient feather."
Karl Häberlein, the German doctor who had bought the skeleton from the owner of the quarry, or perhaps

NETHERLAND

BELGIUM

GERMANY

POLAND

CZECH

FRANCE

X
Solnhofen

accepted it as payment for medical treatment, sold it on to the natural history section of the British Museum in London. The museum paid 860 dollars (700 pounds) for Häberlein's entire collection of Solnhofen fossils, a fortune at the time.

The London specimen, as this particular Archaeopteryx was known, was about the size of a magpie. Most of its head and neck were missing, which made analysis difficult. Professor Richard Owen, a biologist working on the fossil, at first mistook part of the jaw and some teeth for a fossilized fish. But as more and better-preserved fossils of the Archaeopteryx appeared in Bavaria, 12 in total, it became obvious that this type of

ancient bird indeed did have a row of sharp little teeth, unlike the ones living today.

Up until this find, most scientists believed that birds had just suddenly appeared, a type of animal independent of the dinosaurs. (It was the same Professor Owen, by the way, who had come up with the name "dinosaur" in 1842, Greek for "terrible, great lizards.") But now, there was an in-between species, evidence that birds had evolved from dinosaurs.

Archaeopteryx was found just after Charles Darwin had published his highly controversial book "On the Origin of Species", which claimed that different species emerged by a process of natural selection—the successful adaption to the environment—and that humans descended from apes. By providing a link between two kinds of species that were considered unconnected, Archaeopteryx showed that Darwin's idea was right. Birds had indeed evolved from dinosaurs. Later, it was discovered that some dinosaurs that could not fly also had feathers.

But only those who were light and small enough to take flight, like the Archaeopteryx, survived. The others all became extinct 66 million years ago. After that, birds continued to evolve, and they lost their teeth and long, bony tails. But they are now considered surviving dinosaurs. The London specimen can today be seen at the Natural History Museum in London. It is the most valuable fossil in the collection. ✗

THE IMPRINT OF A SINGLE FEATHER WAS FOUND IN 1861, SHORTLY BEFORE THE ARCHAEOPTERYX FOSSIL.

55

The Treasure of the Nibelungen

THE SONG OF THE NIBELUNGS, A GERMAN POEM FROM MEDIEVAL TIMES, TELLS THE STORY OF VALIANT PRINCE SIEGFRIED, WHO KILLED A DRAGON AND BATTLED A DWARF TO WIN A COLOSSAL TREASURE. WHERE IS IT NOW?

At the end of the fourth century, the Roman Empire was breaking up. There were loads of fights all over Central Europe, and many people were on the move in search for a place to live in peace. Historians called this period the "Great Migration." The East Germanic tribe of the Burgundians, for example, resettled in the German city of Worms in 410 after leaving their homes at the Weichsel river in modern-day Poland. But the change of scenery did not work out that well. They were destroyed by the Roman commander Flavius Aetius and an army of Hun soldiers in 436.

This rather tragic tale inspired an unknown author to write an epic poem a good 700 years later. It was called the "Nibelungenlied", "The Song of the Nibelungs" in English. The hero of the poem is Siegfried of Xanten (a town in western Germany), a prince who captures the fabulous treasure of two brothers with funny names—Nibelung and Schibelung— after battling hundreds of enemies, a dwarf called Alberich, and a dragon. Siegfried takes Alberich's magic cape (that makes the wearer invisible and as strong as 12 men) and bathes in the dragon's blood to become invincible.

SOEST X
RHEINBACH X
X GERNSHEIM
X WORMS
RHINE
WEICHSEL

PRINCE SIEGFRIED KILLED
A DRAGON AND PERFORMED
MANY OTHER HEROIC DEEDS.

THE SONG OF THE NIBELUNGS
WAS WRITTEN OVER 800 YEARS AGO.

Or, almost invincible, as we will find out later. The Burgundian king Gunter asked Siegfried to sail with him to Iceland, where Gunter wanted to win the hand of Queen Brünhild. But Brünhild was a very tough and athletic lady. She challenged Gunter to a three-part contest that was a sort of medieval version of sports today. The disciplines were throwing the javelin, throwing a boulder, and a leap. Siegfried put on his cape and secretly helped Gunter to beat Brünhild in the competition. She agreed to marry the king but sensed that something was not quite right.

Back in Worms, Siegfried was allowed to marry Gunter's sister, the lovely princess Kriemhild. Their happiness was short-lived, however. Kriemhild and Brünhild got into fight, and the Queen realized that Siegfried deceived her. The king's vassal, a knight called Hagen, and Brünhild agreed to murder Siegfried. They learned of his weakness: a spot on his shoulder blade that was covered by a linden leaf when he bathed in the dragon's blood. Hagen killed Siegfried with a javelin to his back. As Kriemhild set out to avenge her husband's death by bringing in a foreign army to help, Hagen stole Siegfried's treasure—144 ox carriages of gold—and threw it into the Rhine river for safekeeping. But the exact location of the treasure became a mystery when Hagen and the Burgundians were killed by Attila, the famous Hun king, who married Kriemhild.

While Attila and the Burgundians really existed, Siegfried's adventures were probably made up by the writer of "The Song of the Nibelungs." But that has not stopped treasure hunters from looking for the gold. The search has concentrated on an area near Gernsheim called the "Black Place," where the Rhine makes a sharp turn. Diving expeditions have been unsuccessful, however, and others are convinced that treasure is not buried in the Rhine at all but in a cave in the city of Soest or underneath a field near the village of Rheinbach. ✗

ATTILA THE HUN WAS THE FEARED KING OF WARRIORS THAT INVADED WESTERN EUROPE IN THE FIFTH CENTURY.

SIEGFRIED'S TREASURE WAS SENT AWAY ON CARRIAGES BEFORE IT WAS THROWN INTO THE RHINE RIVER.

The Menorah

THE OLD TESTAMENT TELLS OF A MAGNIFICENT GOLDEN
LAMPSTAND WITH SEVEN LIGHTS IN THE TEMPLE
IN JERUSALEM, WHICH WAS LATER TAKEN TO ROME BY
EMPEROR TITUS. THE MENORAH WAS LOST AFTER
THE VANDALS LOOTED ROME IN 455.

BLACK SEA

CONSTANTINOPLE

ROME

BABYLONE

CARTHAGE

JERUSALEM

MEDITERRANEAN SEA

MENORAH'S TRAVEL

TITUS'S ARMY TOOK THE MENORAH TO ROME.
BUT IT IS UNCLEAR WHERE IT WENT AFTER THAT.

THE MENORAH WAS TAKEN BY THE VANDALS WHEN THEY SACKED ROME IN THE FIFTH CENTURY.

Moses, the bible says, was instructed by god to build a lamp with seven lights to be used in the portable sanctuary, a holy tent that the Israelites carried with them on their 40-year journey from Egypt to the Promised Land. It was lit daily with the finest olive oil. Candles had not been invented yet.

The Menorah or "Light of God" was about 5.3 feet (1.6 meters) high and symbolized the light of wisdom and the creation of the world, which lasted seven days, according to the Old Testament.

But it also had a very practical use. The Temple in Jerusalem, built by King Solomon 300 years after the Exodus from Egypt, had no windows, so the Menorah (and other lamps) were needed to light up the giant building. Electricity had not been invented yet, either.

The original Menorah was most probably stolen by the Egyptian pharaoh Shoshenq, who raided Jerusalem a few decades after it was founded. 400 years later, the Babylonians destroyed the Temple and most of Jerusalem after a three-year siege in 586 BC. The Babylonians took all valuables with them and enslaved the Jewish people. After the return of the Judeans from their 70-year exile and enslavement, the Temple was rebuilt with the permission of Cyrus the Great, the ruler of the Persian Empire who dominated the Middle East at the time. Then Greece became the most powerful nation. The Greek king Antiochus IV Epiphanes outlawed religious practices in Jerusalem and took lamps from the Temple. A new Menorah was most likely built afterwards, and it is that version of the lamp that is depicted on the Arch of Titus in Rome, a relief

from the Roman army's conquest of Jerusalem in 70 BC. The Romans, led by Emperor Titus, had become the latest invaders to pay the Second Temple an unfriendly visit. The arch shows Roman soldiers carrying the Menorah and other artifacts from Jerusalem through the streets of Rome. The Menorah was deposited in the Temple of Peace. But the story does not end there. The Vandals, an East Germanic tribe that had become very mighty and caused a lot of trouble for the Romans, sacked Rome in 455 and took loads of gold and other valuables with them to their capital, Carthage, in North Africa. Did the Menorah make the journey across the Mediterranean?

Did it perhaps sink with some of the boats of the Vandal king Genseric that capsized in a storm? We do not know. One sixth-century historian, Procopius, wrote that the Byzantine (Eastern Roman) army took the Menorah to Constantinople (modern-day Istanbul, Turkey) after defeating the Vandals, and sent the lamp back to Jerusalem. But there is no record of it ever arriving there. In any case, the Persians came back in 614 to destroy Jerusalem once more.

The Menorah has become a symbol of Judaism and is featured on the coat of arms of the state of Israel, founded in 1948. Its fate continues to fascinate. Every year, hundreds of people write to the Vatican, the seat of the Pope in Rome, to ask whether the Menorah is still there, kept in some hidden cellar. Israeli archeologists were invited by the Pope in 2004 to see for themselves but came back none the wiser. ✗

BABYLONIAN KING NEBUCHADNEZZAR II DESTROYED THE FIRST TEMPLE IN 587 BC.

The Priam's Treasure

GERMAN ARCHEOLOGIST HEINRICH SCHLIEMANN FOUND
THE FABLED ANCIENT CITY OF TROY AND A TREASURE
FIT FOR ITS KING, PRIAM. BUT DID IT REALLY BELONG TO HIM?

Heinrich Schliemann was born to poor parents in northeast Germany in 1822, but he had a talent for making money. At 36 he had amassed so much wealth as a businessman, trading everything from Californian gold dust to indigo dye—the color needed to turn fabric blue—that he was able to stop working and devote his life to his passion. He wanted to find Troy, the scene of the Trojan War from Homer's classical

tale the "Iliad", one of the most famous texts in Greek mythology—a mixture of real history and fairytale. According to Homer, the war started after Paris, the prince of Troy, stole Helen, the wife of King Menelaus of Sparta. Menelaus's brother, King Agamemnon, laid siege to Troy in revenge. After 10 years, the Greeks finally succeed in taking the city by hiding soldiers inside a wooden horse that the Trojans had rather stupidly accepted as a gift. The Greek king Odysseus had come up with that clever ruse.

KING PRIAM WAS THE RULER OF TROY, THE CITY CAPTURED BY THE GREEKS WITH THE HELP OF THE TROJAN HORSE.

In the nineteenth century, most people believed that the Trojan War was just an old story. But Schliemann was sure the events Homer described were what really happened. He went to Hisarlik, a city in the northeast of the Ottoman Empire (modern-day Turkey) that some believed to be the site of Troy, and started digging there in 1871, using dynamite sticks to smash through several layers of old rubble. When he reached the remnants of a heavy wall, he stopped. He thought he had found Troy.

Two years later, he was even more certain that he was in the right spot. Schliemann had uncovered a hoard of gold jewelry and other precious artifacts he believed to be the treasure of King Priam. Schliemann smuggled the find out of the country. He had his wife, Sophia, wear a wonderful diadem, earrings, and chains—a set he called the Jewels of Helen—in public.
But later excavations proved that Schliemann had made a mistake. At least nine cities had been built at

HEINRICH SCHLIEMANN'S WIFE, SOPHIA, WORE THE ANCIENT JEWELRY IN PUBLIC.

Hisarlik, one on top of the other, and the German had dug far too deep, to very old settlements from the Bronze Age. The Troy of the "Iliad" was several layers higher up, more than 1,000 years later in time. Its ruins were dated to 1184 BC and showed signs of war and willful destruction. Schliemann's unsophisticated methods have done much to damage the site. Most archeologists agree, however, that Homer's Troy once really stood at Hisarlik. But the treasure of Priam most certainly belonged to a different wealthy man or woman, as it is about 1,000 years older. Parts of these beautiful works of ancient craftsmen can today be seen in the Istanbul Archeology Museums, with the rest on display in the Pushkin Museum in Moscow as of 1993. It was brought there from the Royal Museums in Berlin by Red Army soldiers at the end of the Second World War. The Russian government has refused to return the treasure to Germany, saying that it compensates Russia for the war damage caused by the Germans. ✗

SCHLIEMANN THOUGHT THE TREASURE BELONGED TO KING PRIAM, BUT IT TURNED OUT TO BE MUCH OLDER.

67

The Tomb of Genghis Khan

THE MONGOLIAN LEADER GENGHIS KHAN, THE FOUNDER OF THE LARGEST EMPIRE IN HUMAN HISTORY, WAS BURIED IN SECRET, TOGETHER WITH FANTASTICAL RICHES FROM HIS MANY CONQUESTS. WILL HIS TOMB EVER BE FOUND?

Before he became a feared warlord who conquered large parts of Asia and Eastern Europe in the twelfth and thirteenth centuries, Genghis Khan was just a simple boy called Temüjin. Temüjin was born in 1162 and his family had a hard life as nomads, constantly traveling through the Mongolian wilderness. When he was nine years old, the Tatars, a tribe that were the enemies of the Mongolians, killed Temüjin's father with poisoned food.

For a while, Temüjin and his brothers were so poor that they had to hunt small animals such as marmots—large squirrels that probably did not taste nice—and eat the decayed meat of dead cattle—which definitely did not taste nice—to survive.

Temüjin was captured by another tribe and made to work as a slave, with his head locked in a block of wood. But he escaped, rejoined his brothers, and set out to raise an army to avenge his father's death. Temüjin was very smart and very ruthless. He convinced other Mongolian tribes to join him and destroyed the Tatars, killing anyone taller than three feet (one meter), even young children.

His army kept growing with every successful battle. His soldiers were very organized, orchestrating their attacks with flags, drums, and flares.

AFTER A VERY UNHAPPY CHILDHOOD, GENGHIS KHAN GREW UP TO BE ONE OF THE MOST FEARSOME WARLORDS IN HISTORY.

-1267-

MONGOLIA

THE MONGOLIAN ARMY CONQUERED ALL OF CENTRAL ASIA, AS WELL AS PARTS OF EUROPE AND CHINA.

They could fire arrows while riding horses, and Temüjin made sure that there was always enough food around. In 1206, Temüjin had become so powerful that all Mongolians agreed to proclaim him Genghis Khan, the ruler of everybody. He was also declared the representative of the supreme Mongolian god, Mongke Koko Tengri

("Eternal Blue Sky"). To follow him was now a religious duty.

Genghis Khan conquered most of China, Siberia, all of Central Asia, and parts of India and Eastern Europe, destroying cities and killing hundreds of thousands of people. His territory stretched from the Sea of Japan in the East to the Caspian Sea in the West. The Mongolian Empire was expanded by his sons and grandsons into the Middle East and Central Europe, all the way to the outskirts of Vienna in Austria.

Genghis Khan died aged 63. Depending on who you believe, he either fell off his horse, had a problem breathing, or was killed by an arrow in battle in China. He was buried near his birthplace in northern Mongolia with six live cats—so that their purrs could guide him to the afterlife—and heaps of gold. His grave was unmarked, however, and he instructed his soldiers to further hide it by diverting a river over it or by planting trees. There are also reports that all witnesses to the burial were killed to make sure the location remained a secret.

Many people have tried to find his tomb over the centuries. There are suggestions that Khan is buried near the Burkhan Khaldun mountain, in an area the Mongols called the "Great Taboo" or the "Forbidden." But the search has been hampered by the Mongolian's belief that the soil is sacred and must not be disturbed. Since 2015, new efforts have made use of advanced satellite and drone technology. More than 10,000 volunteers have joined in the hunt to find the resting place of one the world's greatest warriors. ✘

SIX LIVE CATS WERE BURIED WITH GENGHIS KHAN TO GUIDE HIM TO THE AFTERLIFE WITH THEIR PURRS.

The Ark of the Covenant

ACCORDING TO THE OLD TESTAMENT, GOD INSTRUCTED THE ISRAELITES TO CONSTRUCT A GOLD-COVERED WOODEN BOX TO HOUSE MOSES'S TWO STONE TABLETS OF THE TEN COMMANDMENTS. THE ARK HAS BEEN MISSING SINCE THE BABYLONIANS DESTROYED THE TEMPLE OF JERUSALEM IN 587 BC.

TWO ANGEL-LIKE CREATURES SAT ON TOP OF THE GOLDEN ARK.

One of the most interesting stories told by the Hebrew bible is the Exodus, the desert journey of the Israelites to the Promised Land after escaping slavery in Egypt. (The bible says they had been forced to build the pyramids there but there is no historical evidence for that.) 12 months into their 40-year trip—they did not have a good satnav, unfortunately—their leader, Moses, came down from Mount Sinai with the Ten Commandments and a very detailed manual for building an ark, on direct orders from god. The vessel was known as the Ark of the Covenant because of god's covenant with the Israelites, a promise to look after them if they adhered to his laws. A box made of acacia wood, covered with a layer of gold and with two angel-like winged figures on its lid, was made to contain the stone tablets, and was carried by members of one of the 12 Jewish tribes, the Levites, ahead of the people when on the march. The Ark, covered by blue cloth, was also said to contain a pot of manna, the food that god helpfully provided every day in the desert, which

Jerusalem

IRAK

× Mount
△ Nebo
△

× Babylon

EGYPT

Medina
×

× Mekka

× Axum

ETHIOPIA

THE ARK WAS LOST WHEN THE
BABYLONIANS DESTROYED THE TEMPLE OF
JERUSALEM IN 587 BC.

apparently tasted of whatever somebody wanted it to taste of. Yum! In
addition, the wooden rod of Moses's
brother, Aaron, a nifty magic stick that
could turn into a snake or an almond
tree, was placed into the Ark, too.
A few years later, the Ark was captured by a foreign enemy called the
Philistines after a battle. But the bible
says that god punished the Philistines
with a plague of mice and itchy
bumps, so they happily returned it to
the Israelites, along with some gold to
apologize for any inconvenience

caused. In the days of King Solomon,
who was famous for being a very
wise man, the Ark was moved into the
Temple of Jerusalem (970-931 BC)
and rested in a special, secret chamber
called the Holy of Holies for almost
400 years. But then came the
Babylonians. King Nebuchadnezzar II
invaded Jerusalem, destroyed the
Temple in 587 BC, and the Ark vanished. Some say it was dismantled and
taken back to Babylon (modern-day
Iraq), while others contend that it was
buried deep inside the Temple Mount

or on Mount Nebo, near the Jordan River, to protect it from the looting foreign army.

Dozens of different theories have sprung up over the Ark's location, if indeed it ever existed. Since the Temple Mount is also holy to Muslims—the Al-Aqsa Mosque and Dome of the Rock were built in the same location in the seventh century—no wide-scale excavations have taken place there in modern times. People have looked to Ancient Rome and even as far as Ireland and France to find it, while Orthodox Christians in Ethiopia actually believe that Menelik, the son of King Solomon and the Queen of Sheba (who had traveled to Jerusalem to trade spices from her kingdom in present-day Yemen), took it with him to East Africa well before the Babylonians invaded. They claim that it is being kept in a church in the Ethiopian city of Axum today, where only one monk, the so-called "guardian of the Ark," is allowed to see it. Maybe he could post a picture of it on the internet? ✗

The Bactrian Gold

*20,000 PIECES OF ANCIENT JEWELRY BELONGING TO
A NOMADIC TRIBE WITH VERY FLASHY TASTE
WERE FOUND IN AFGHANISTAN IN 1978. THE TREASURE
HAD TO STAY HIDDEN IN A VAULT FOR 25 YEARS
TO ESCAPE THE ATTENTION OF SOME VERY BAD PEOPLE.*

The little mount outside the northern Afghanistan town of Sheberghan did not look like much. But locals knew something immensely valuable was buried there. They called it Tillya Tepe, the "hill of gold." In the winter of 1978, archeologists from the neighboring Soviet Union—as Communist Russia was called then—proved the locals right. They unearthed more than 20,000 items of gold that

had been buried with their former owners: coins, jewelry, a statuette of the Greek goddess of love and beauty, Aphrodite, a crown, belt buckles, animals, mirrors, parts of clothing, and even golden sandals (that cannot have been very comfortable). The sheer variety of the pieces dug up showed that many different cultures from far away places, such as China, India, and Greece, had met and traded goods with each other in this remote area in Central Asia.

The Kushan nomads who owned these fabulously expensive items lived around the time of Christ and obviously loved to show off. One would have seen them coming from a mile away, with all their gold glistening in the Afghani desert sun.

The Bactrian gold, as it came to be known, was given over to the National Museum in Afghanistan's capital, Kabul. In 1979, the hoard survived the invasion of the Soviet Union's Red Army—they had intervened in a civil war on behalf of Afghanistan's communist government, their allies—but an insurgence by Afghan fighters and others hoping to get rid of the Russians brought chaos to Kabul a decade later. In 1989, it was decided that the museum's priceless artifacts should be

BEAUTIFUL STATUETTES OF ANIMALS AND GODS AS WELL AS FINE JEWELRY ARE PART OF THE TREASURE.

hidden in the vaults of the Central Bank inside the presidential palace to keep it safe from thieves. Workers involved in transferring the goods vowed to keep the secret.

The bad times in Afghanistan got worse. In 1996, an extremely violent group of religious fanatics, the Taliban, took control of the country. The Taliban destroyed many archeological treasures because they do not allow the depiction of living things. They also demanded to be shown the contents of the Central Bank vault.

An employee reluctantly opened the safe door. The Taliban counted the gold bars and money, then left again. The employee closed the door and turned the key the wrong way on purpose. It snapped, leaving the lock broken. The Taliban did not notice.

Five years later, in November 2001, the Taliban were about to be driven out of Afghanistan by the American army and their allies. A group of Taliban leaders went to the Central Bank. They stole millions of dollars and precious stones from safes and deposit

THE TALIBAN TRIED TO STEAL THE TREASURE IN 2001 BUT WERE TRICKED BY A BANK EMPLOYEE.

boxes before fleeing the country, but all their attempts to open the door of the presidential vault had failed. The lock was still jammed.

Following Kabul's liberation, things quietened down. Still, nobody had seen the Bactrian gold. As local locksmiths managed to at last open the vault door in August 2002, Afghan president Hamid Karzai found gold bars and cash worth 110 million dollars (85 million pounds). But the ancient treasure of the Kushans was not there. As it turned out, workers from the museum had hidden it in ordinary-looking trunks under another set of crates in one of the upper floors of the bank. The Taliban had simply missed it. Today, the Bactrian gold is back on show at the National Museum in Kabul. ✗

The Terracotta Army

WHEN THE FIRST EMPEROR OF CHINA DIED IN 210 BC, HE DID NOT WANT TO HEAD INTO THE AFTERLIFE ALONE. AN ARMY OF 8,000 CLAY SOLDIERS WAS BURIED NEAR HIM TO KEEP HIM COMPANY.

All of his life, Qin Shi Huang, the first emperor of China, was worried about death. One of his earliest decisions as a ruler—he was only 13 years old at the time—was to instruct the building of his mausoleum, a 250-foot-tall (76-meter-tall) mound to house his tomb. He was just a very negative person.

Qin Shi Huang was constantly afraid people were out to murder him. He was very superstitious and did not trust anybody. He built a section of the Great Wall of China to keep his enemies out of the north and ordered his doctors to concoct a magical elixir that would bestow eternal life. Unfortunately for him, the pills they created contained mercury (quicksilver), a highly poisonous metal. He swallowed some and died soon after, aged 49, on September 10, 210 BC. As it was, he had had good reason to be suspicious of those close to him. Li Si, the prime minister, and another government official agreed to murder Qin Shi Huang's son Fusu, who was supposed to be the next emperor, and put his younger brother Hu Hai on the throne instead.

2,183 years later, in March 1974, a farmer called Yang Zhifa dug for a well one mile (1.6 kilometers) east of Qin Shi Huang's tomb, outside Xi'an, a city in Central China. After three days, he hit a structure made from terracotta, a ceramic made of fired clay. Zhifa thought he had found an

QUIN SHI HUANG BUILT AN UNDERGROUND CITY WITH CLAY PEOPLE TO KEEP HIM COMPANY AFTER DEATH.

8,000 CLAY SOLDIERS SILENTLY STAND GUARD AT THE EMPEROR'S TOMB.

old oven, but further digging revealed the body of a soldier, missing his head and a leg. Zhifa told the authorities. Archeologists came and slowly uncovered an entire army — 8,000 clay soldiers, 130 chariots with 520 horses, and 150 cavalry horses — that had been buried 16 feet (five meters) underground to guard the emperor's tomb. Each soldier had a unique facial expression, his own weapon, and stood ordered by rank.

Some of the real weapons the soldiers held in their hands — swords, spears, lances, battle axes, crossbows — were stolen by grave robbers shortly after the burial, hundreds of years ago, but many were still there. The silent soldiers were originally painted to make them look as if they were alive. Unfortunately, the lacquer quickly peeled off after they were exposed. The Terracotta Army only takes up part of what is a detailed underground

CHINA

QIN
× Xianyang

version of Qin Shi Huang's empire, stretching thousands of miles in all directions. Further digs have found bronze statues of animals, the walls of a model of the Imperial Palace, and clay representations of the people who served at the emperor's court: musicians, butlers, acrobats, and jesters. It makes you wonder what kind of jokes they told to cheer up grumpy old Qin Shi Huang.

The tomb of the emperor itself is roughly the size of a football pitch but has not yet been opened. There are concerns that the artifacts it holds could be damaged by exposure, just like the soldiers, and also worries over very high levels of toxic mercury that have been measured there. Apparently, the creators of the mausoleum used the liquid metal to recreate rivers and lakes.

Millions come to see the Terracotta Army each year, and some of the soldiers have gone on tour, getting displayed in museums around the world. At the British Museum in London, for example, the emperor's clay warriors were the most popular archeological exhibition since the treasures from Tutankhamun's tomb were shown there in 1972. ✗

COLORFUL PAINT MADE THE SOLDIERS LOOK VERY REALISTIC BUT IT PEELED OFF AFTER EXPOSURE TO THE AIR.

THE CLAY SOLDIERS CARRY REAL WEAPONS THAT WERE USED AT THE TIME.

MAHARAJA SREE CHITHIRA THIRUNAL BALARAMA VARMA ORDERED THE OPENING OF ONE VAULT IN 1931.

The Padmanabhaswamy Temple

IT HAD LONG BEEN KNOWN THAT THE VAULTS OF A HINDU TEMPLE CONTAINED MASSES OF GOLD. BUT THE ASTRONOMICAL RICHES INVESTIGATORS UNCOVERED IN 2011 DEFIED ALL EXPECTATIONS...

Padmanabhaswamy Temple in Kerala, southern India, is dedicated to Vishnu, one of three principal gods in Hinduism. Vishnu, who is said to protect the world in times of danger and chaos, is depicted in the temple as sleeping peacefully on the serpent Adishesha, his servant on earth. The deity is made from 12,000 pieces of fossilized black shells. Sridevi-Lakshmi, the goddess of prosperity (good fortune), and the goddess of earth, Bhudevi, are next to Vishnu. Nobody knows when the temple was built. It is that old. But it was already described as the "Golden Temple" over 2,000 years ago, due to the unimaginable wealth amassed there. Many rulers of India, kings from near and far, as well as ordinary people, have donated valuables to Vishnu, and all of it has been stored in the underground vaults that only the temple priests have been allowed to enter.

For about 400 years, the former royal family of India, the Travancores, acted as the temple's administrators and guarded its secrets. One attempt to retrieve valuables from one of the cellars (Vault B) in 1908 ended with angry cobras chasing away the explorers. They ran away very quickly, an observer noted. Just over 30 years later, gold supplies in India ran so low that the outer chamber of Vault B was opened on the orders of a Travancore family member, the Maharaja Sree Chithira Thirunal Balarama Varma. The gold in Vault B was considered the personal property of the Travancore family rather than of the temple itself.

Concerns over the proper handling of the incredible treasure led to the Supreme Court of India deciding that the contents of the vaults should be listed in an official inventory in 2011. For the first time ever, outsiders were allowed to open four of the eight vaults. What they found was scarcely believable: a veritable mountain of gold and precious items from all over the world, dating back to antiquity. 2,100 different groups of objects were retrieved, including coins from

ANGRY COBRAS JEALOUSLY GUARD THE MOUNTAINS OF GOLD IN THE TEMPLE VAULT.

the Roman Empire and from the time of Napoleon, three golden crowns, a golden throne covered with diamonds and gemstones, thousands of gold chains, sacks full of precious stones, necklaces and diadems, a golden idol of the god Mahavishnu, and even golden coconut shells with diamonds as an adornment. Estimates put the total value at 22 billion dollars. That is 22,000 million dollars (17,000 million pounds). But that is just the physical value of the gold and gemstones.

If all these historical artifacts were up for sale, collectors might pay 10 times as much. And remember: half of the eight temple vaults have not even been opened yet. It is hard to imagine how much more gold—and how many more angry cobras—could be found there. Whichever way you look at it, Padmanabhaswamy Temple is truly extraordinary: it is by far the wealthiest place of worship of any kind in the recorded history of the world. ✘

The Nuestra Señora de Atocha

AMERICAN TREASURE HUNTER MEL FISHER SPENT
DECADES LOOKING FOR THE SHIPWRECK OF A SPANISH
GALLEON, BATTLING HARDSHIP AND PERSONAL TRAGEDY.
ONE DAY IN JULY 1985, FISHER GOT LUCKY.

THE LOSS OF THE ATOCHA
SERIOUSLY HURT KING
PHILIP IV OF SPAIN'S POCKET.

The heavily armed Nuestra Señora de Atocha ("Our Lady of Atocha") was the most important ship of a fleet of Spanish vessels carrying riches from the New World (Central and South America) across the Atlantic in September 1622. The Atocha's treasure alone (silver, gold, precious emeralds) was so enormous that it had taken two entire months to bring it onboard at the port in Panama.

After a last stop in Havana (today's capital of Cuba), the Atocha and its convoy of ships were hit by a severe hurricane 35 miles (55 kilometers) west of Key West. The Atocha lost its sail and rudder, then was slammed into a reef by a huge wave. The 112-foot-long (34-meter-long) galleon quickly sank with 80 tons of precious cargo in waters 55 feet (17 meters) deep. Only five of the 265-strong crew, three sailors and two slaves, survived by tying themselves to a mast.

King Philip IV of Spain sent ships to recover the treasure with the help of diving bells and slaves. He really needed the money. Spain was fighting other European powers in the Thirty Years' War at the time, a battle between Catholics and Protestants that cost millions of lives and was very expensive. As the name suggests, it lasted for 30 years and devastated most of Germany, where most of the battles took place. Philip IV, whose army fought on the side of the Catholics, was soon forced to borrow extra money to finance the conflict because his men only found the wreck of the Margarita, another vessel from the same fleet. The Atocha treasure had been scattered over a very wide area by the hurricane. Only the odd coin was reclaimed.

More than 300 years later, Mel Fisher, a former chicken farmer from the U.S. state of Indiana, moved to California to open a diving school with his wife, Dolores. Dolores set a record for staying more than two whole days (50 hours) underwater, and she shared Mel's passion for finding sunken treasure. Together with their five children, Terry, Dirk, Kim, and Kane, and daughter Taffi, they relocated to Florida in 1969 to start the search for the Atocha.

For many years, the Fishers found nothing but hard times and sorrow in the turquoise waters off Key West. In 1975, the oldest son, Dirk Fisher, his wife, Angel, and a diver died

MEL FISHER AND HIS WIFE, DOLORES, SPENT 26 YEARS HUNTING THE ATOCHA TREASURE.

when water penetrated their boat. But even this tragedy could not stop Mel continuing his quest. "Today's the day!" he would tell himself, over and over. And on July 20, 1985, his day finally came.

Kane Fisher was the first to spot the wreck of Atocha, near the Marquesas Keys, a group of islands 12 miles (20 kilometers) west of Key West. The Fishers found tons of metal coins minted in the sixteenth and seventeenth centuries and several kilograms of the finest emeralds, green gemstones from Bolivia. One emerald ring alone was worth 500,000 dollars (390,000 pounds). In total, the treasure was worth 450 million dollars (350 million pounds). "The shipwreck of the century," the newspapers called it.

Every year, 36 hobby divers are invited by two of Mel Fisher's grandsons to take part in the search for the Atocha's sterncastle, a section at the back of the ship that has not been discovered yet and is estimated to contain 400 silver bars and 130,000 silver coins worth at least 500 million dollars (390 million pounds). One day, it could be your day, too. ✗

THE SHIPWRECK WAS FOUND OFF THE COAST OF FLORIDA, USA.

GULF OF MEXICO

MIAMI

KEY WEST

✗ ATOCHA

HAVANA

The Rosetta Stone

FOR HUNDREDS OF YEARS, NO ONE COULD UNDERSTAND HIEROGLYPHICS, THE WRITTEN LANGUAGE USED BY THE PHARAOHS IN EGYPT—UNTIL A SOLDIER IN NAPOLEON'S ARMY FOUND A STONE THAT PROVED TO BE THE KEY TO DECIPHERING THE ANCIENT CODE.

WHEN NAPOLEON INVADED EGYPT IN 1798, HE BROUGHT SCIENTISTS WITH HIM TO STUDY THE ANCIENT EGYPTIAN CULTURE.

Napoleon Bonaparte was a short man with a big appetite for conquering the world. Before crowning himself emperor in 1804, he was a successful general who fought in a series of wars after the French Revolution of 1789. One of his military expeditions took him to Egypt in 1798. Napoleon's aim was to disrupt the British trade route with India. The British were his fiercest enemy. Napoleon's army was joined by a group of scientific experts eager to uncover the secrets of the pyramids, and the Institut d'Égypte for the scientific study of Ancient Egypt was founded in Cairo. One year after the French had landed in the country, a French lieutenant called Pierre-François Bouchard noticed that one of the stones his men had used to strengthen the walls of Fort Julien, a few miles outside (several kilometers) the port city of Rosetta (Rashid in

THE STONE ORIGINALLY STOOD IN A TEMPLE OF GRECO-EGYPTIAN KING PTOLEMY V. HIS IMAGE IS IMPRINTED ON ANCIENT COINS.

modern-day Egypt), looked very peculiar. It was made of dark grey granite and contained incomplete inscriptions of three types: Ancient Greek, hieroglyphics (the writing system of Ancient Egypt), and Demotics, another written version of the old Egyptian language.

The stone was sent to the Institut d'Égypt where it was correctly suggested that it contained three versions of the same text. Napoleon himself was able to inspect it before heading home to France.

The French army in Egypt was defeated by the British two years later. The Rosetta Stone, as it was already known then, passed into the hands of King George III, who ordered the stone to be delivered to the British Museum, where it is still on display today. Prints of the inscriptions were made and sent to scholars all over Europe to help with the translation.

Starting from the Greek text, the scientists discovered that the Rosetta Stone was a fragment of a larger, 6.5-feet-tall (2-meter-tall) stone called a stela that once stood in a religious temple. It contained a message from a group of Egyptian priests from 196 BC that declared that the Greco-Egyptian king Ptolemy V,